Playing With Your Dog

Playing With Your Dog

Have a Smarter, Fitter, Happier Dog

Hanne Grice

Library of Congress Control Number:		2010909558
ISBN:	Hardcover	978-1-4535-2965-2
	Softcover	978-1-4535-2964-5
	Ebook	978-1-4535-2966-9

This book was printed in the United States of America.

To order additional copies of this book, contact:
Xlibris Corporation
0-800-644-6988
www.xlibrispublishing.co.uk
Orders@xlibrispublishing.co.uk
300594

Contents

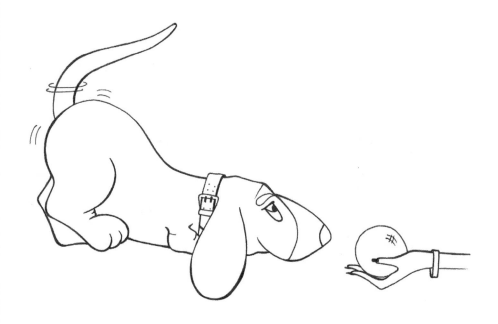

Introduction

The first things we learn are learnt through playing—that bouncy red ball that escaped you so many times at the beach was the key to developing the coordination that lets you eat food, tie your shoelaces, and even fly a jet aircraft.

As we grow up, we play less and less, but when we remember the adage about 'all work and no play' and go outside with a ball, we feel revived and enthusiastic. Your dog is only too happy to help you feel like this all the time.

According to the theory of Neoteny, which looks at how some genetic variants retain juvenile characteristics into adulthood, one of the reasons why we enjoy the company of dogs so much is because they are playful throughout their lives. Playing is fun for you and it is fun for your dog. Playing also helped us to make friends and it can help you bond with your dog too. You may even find that they share your love of football, tennis, or tug of war, even if they don't have a great grasp of the rules. More importantly, just as it did for you, playing can help your dog in other ways. It allows your dog to use its natural behaviours by boosting its fitness and cognitive skills. Dogs, like children, learn to play at a young age. Research by the psychologist and dog expert, Dr Stanley Coren, found that the average dog is smarter than the human toddler and it is true that if you give a puppy (or a child) a cardboard box, they can play with it for hours. By nurturing this playfulness in your dog and using his natural behaviours, this will be rewarding for both you and your dog. This book will help you work out the games that are best suited for your dog to play throughout his life, from puppyhood to old age.

Play School

As our lives become much busier, many owners struggle to find time to play with their dog and may place greater value on walking their pet as a way of providing exercise, while others may worry that if they start a game with their dog, it will go on and on for an hour. However, even just ten minutes of direct attention through play can go a long way to satisfying your dog. Dogs learn through play from a very young age, finding out about their limits while still with their littermates. By two weeks of age, the young puppy will have touch reflexes on his front legs and by three weeks, on his back legs, which help him explore and solve problems. During this time, the puppy also learns how to regulate his bite through playing with his littermates and mother by biting and being bitten back. The behaviourist, John Fisher, said, 'The only purpose these needle sharp teeth have is to cause pain'. Your puppy will be well aware of the impact his bite has after playing with his siblings. Playing with the litter helps to create social bonds with other dogs and it affects and moulds adult social behaviour, as the rough and tumble games teach the puppy important communication skills. Play predicts the future status of the pups within the pack—which ones have stronger personalities and which pups are more submissive. The mother's role is to teach them the survival skills of hunting, pouncing, and shaking their prey—actions they will continue to hone throughout their lives. However, if your dog is deprived of play, it may suffer from physiological and behavioural problems. Studies have proved that monotonous, unchanging, and unchallenging environments lead to boredom and abnormal behaviour patterns (displaying signs similar to depression and lethargy).

A study conducted by the University of Illinois took a group of overweight, elderly rats out of standard laboratory cages and put them into an exciting, new environment, which included swings, slides, toys, and hanging objects. These rats became more active, lost weight, and had an increased number of cerebellar synapses compared to the unstimulated group of rats. This proved that individual nerve cells are capable of growing new connections even in an older animal through exercising and stimulating the brain.

A Clever Canine

If studies have proven that an environment rich in stimulation together with a combination of a well-balanced diet improves brain function in dogs, can we therefore turn our dog into a 'Canine Einstein' through play? The answer is yes! Harvard psychologist, Howard Gardener, categorised dog's intelligence into specific kinds: observational and social learning, environmental learning, spacial awareness, instinctive and linguistic intelligence, and the dog's personality. Playing can actually test and enhance your dog's spacial awareness, memory, problem-solving abilities, observational skills, and linguistic understanding whatever his age. In addition, by playing with your dog, you become much more interesting and important to your four-legged friend, helping him become more focused and responsive to you. What could be better than that?

A great example of a game that tests your dog's spatial intelligence is 'hide and seek'. When my husband and I play this with our dog Howard, I will say, 'Where's Daddy?' while my husband is concealed behind a tree. Howard will run to where he last saw Daddy and then show excitement and bark on finding Daddy as a signal to me.

Owners may see their dog displaying spatial intelligence when their dog remembers where they left their toy or that very important buried bone. Studies show that dogs learn to map their environment by memorising where things are relative to certain prominent landmarks. However, if these landmarks are moved or removed, the dogs make errors in trying to locate things, much the same as humans. A study by Nicole Chapuis in 1983 observed dogs navigating around different types of obstacles. Chapuis varied the visibility of the food (using opaque barriers), the distance to reach the target, and the angular deviation required at the initiation of the route. The experiment illustrated that if the target was hidden behind the screens, the dogs showed a preference for taking the most optimal route. The visibility of the target modified the dogs' orientation such that they tried to maintain a direction which deviated to a lesser degree from the target. Therefore, the target acted like a 'perceptual anchor'. Centuries ago, animals were thought to be without consciousness, intelligence, or thoughts. Charles Darwin challenged such beliefs and studies have found that the roots of cognition are deep, widespread, and fluid. New mental skills can evolve and this is illustrated by a dog's ability to understand human forms of communication.

Rico-Dog of Letters In 2001, a Border collie called Rico made a name for himself appearing on a German television game show, because of his knowledge of the names of over two hundred toys and skill in learning new ones. The Max Planck Institute for Evolutionary Anthropology studied Rico and, in one test, he used deduction to 'fetch the bunny', despite it being an unfamiliar phrase. He went through a process of elimination and worked out that since he knew the names of the other toys, this 'bunny' must be the unfamiliar object.

Dogs also have their own language, using visual signals (body language) and voice. Adam Miklosi at the Eotvos University in Budapest conducted tests by hiding a dog's favourite toy or piece of food in one of three locations in the absence of the dog's owner. When the owners returned, Miklosi found that the restrained dogs showed their owners where the desired object had been placed by first barking to get their attention and then looking back and forth between the object's location and the owners. Most dog owners may see similar behaviour displayed by their dog when it rolls its ball under the sofa and cannot get to it. Dr Coren, who found that the average dog is smarter than a human toddler, demonstrated that dogs can count, reason, and recognise approximately 165 words, as well as understanding gestures like pointing and non-verbal sounds, such as whistles. He also worked with two hundred dog-obedience judges to rank 110 breeds based on their intelligence levels. Border collies, poodles, retrievers, German shepherds, and Doberman pinschers were among the dogs ranked highly with cases like Rico supporting such findings. In contrast, bulldogs, chow chows, borzoi, and Afghan hounds were bottom of the class. However, it's not as simple as the results imply. Collies and retrievers have been selectively bred through generations to hone their skills to humans' needs. Dogs natural behaviours such as hunting do not need any honing, so there has been no need for them to learn linguistic skills. Dr Coren's research teaches us that once you understand what your dog hones into, you can create games which are much more stimulating than simply throwing a ball.

The Nature of Play

To understand what games your dog will find most satisfying, you need to understand his natural behaviours. It will also help you understand why your Jack Russell, who is bred to dig out rodents, enjoys digging up your prize roses, while next door's retriever leaves their garden alone. The range of dog's natural behaviours are:

- scenting
- tracking
- stalking
- chasing
- pouncing
- biting/killing
- mounting
- barking
- digging
- regurgitation
- territorial guarding
- chewing/gnawing

Some of these behaviours are less welcome than others in a domestic setting, but your dog will use most of them in play.

A Sense of Play

All of your dog's senses are also crucial to their enjoyment of games.

Smell

Your dog has an incredible nose. The average human has five million hair cells up their nose and your dog has over 220 million. The average dog has such acutely sensitive scenting ability that it can identify smells so diluted that even scientific instruments cannot measure them. To study this, John Paul Scott and John L. Fuller placed untrained beagles, Fox terriers, and Scottie dogs in a one-acre field and released a mouse. It took the beagles around a minute to locate the mouse and the terriers fifteen minutes. The Scotties never found the mouse.

> **Sense Games** 'Hide and seek', 'hunt the treat', 'sniff out supper', and 'what cup is it under?' all use your dog's sense of smell.

Taste

Although your dog's sense of smell is much more developed than yours, we have much better taste. Where the human mouth contains approximately nine thousand taste buds, a dog's mouth has only 1,706. Taste buds are located mainly on the tongue and help to distinguish four qualities: sweet, sour, bitter, and salt. All other tastes are detected by olfactory receptors located high in our nasal passages. As dogs demonstrate taste preferences, it is likely that they can also detect the four qualities of sweet, sour, bitter, and salt. It is likely that having fewer taste buds means they have less ability to detect subtleties.

It is thought that dogs have additional primary taste receptors (like cats) that can respond to water, allowing them to taste different types of water. Although humans will resist eating something that smells bad, dogs are the opposite—the smellier, the better. As dogs are opportunist feeders, and because their survival mechanism is so great, if there is a food source available, they will take it, so don't be harsh on your dog if he swipes your cheese sandwich from the table when your back is turned.

> **Sense Games** Use a variety of foods, varying in size and textures. A dog is much more likely to work harder for higher value rewards than bits of kibble. You can also put them in containers or shop-bought toys like Kongs, Buster Cubes, and puzzle games.

Hearing

Our dogs, like us, have special areas in the brain that control specific activities. The dog's ear is divided into three parts: the outer ear (pinna), the middle, and the inner ear. The inner ear is housed in the temporal bone and is the most complicated part of the ear. It is divided into two systems, which deal with hearing and balance. Although loud noises can stimulate a response from a newborn puppy, it is not until he is about twelve to fourteen days old that his external ear canals open and a clear response to a loud noise is evident.

P. W. B. Joslin believed that dogs can hear approximately four times the distance that humans can. However, some psychologists, including Dr Coren, believe that for some sounds, a dog's hearing is hundreds of times better than ours. Dogs have a greater range and can hear ultrasound, which is above our capacity, as well as sounds of low frequency. A study of grey wolves led to veterinarian Bruce Fogle concluding that this ability allows wolves to hear small prey, such as mice.

> **Sense Games** The ability to differentiate between a wide range of sounds, such as tone of voice, a dog whistle, and tongue clicks means that you can teach your dog to link different actions to different sounds, as sheepdogs do.

Sight

We see things differently to our dogs. Our brain has more neurons to process and transmit sight information than any of our other senses. We therefore interpret the environment based on what we see more than what we smell, hear, taste, or touch. Dogs, however, are led by what they smell, taste, and touch.

Look at your dog and you will notice that his eyes are placed more to the side of his head, compared to yours, which are at the front. This means they have a greater panoramic view of the world, helping them with hunting and survival. It is suggested that dogs can see at twenty feet what a normal human can see clearly at seventy-five feet.

Although your dog will track his prey with his sense of smell, his sense of sight confirms his trail when it gets close enough. Once his prey is in motion, it is easier for your dog to track, which is why many prey animals will freeze as a way to elude the dog.

> **Sense Games** Games such as 'fetch', using multiple toys, or 'tag' make use of this sense.

Touch

This is one of the most important senses but is also the most overlooked. It enables us to determine if something is warm or cold, helps us respond to pain as well as light touch and deep pressure. Touch does more than just detect physical contact with our body; it helps us have an understanding of our environment.

Early in life, our brain and bodies rely on the sense of touch to enable us to grow. Research suggests that babies who are touched grow and develop a lot faster than if they are not and the same is true of our dogs. A newborn puppy will use his taste reflexes and nerves to sense the warmth of his mother and any movements away from her will cause the puppy to experience a temperature drop, leading him to vocalise his distress until he is rescued by his mother. It is also touch and taste that enable the puppy to locate the mother's nipple to have that all-important meal. Because touch is a sense that is generally well developed at birth, many have suggested that it is possibly the most important of all the canine senses and is extremely important for the development of a mature and sensible mind. Research has also indicated that puppies raised in isolation do not seem to know how to avoid painful stimuli and may even perceive pain differently. Understanding your dog's reaction and 'touch sensitivity' is very important and is often taken into consideration when testing a young dog's temperament and aptitude. Behaviourists, such as Joachim and Wendy Volhard, Clarence Pfaffenberger, Fortunate Fields, and William Campell, developed tests that include reaction to touch and suggested that a dog that is too sensitive to touch may be harder to handle and train. Often owners want to play 'rough and tumble' games with their dog or even hug their dog as a way of demonstrating their friendship and love. However, some dogs may not enjoy such physical contact especially those sensitive to touch, while other dogs enjoy being stroked and petted. It is important to remember that only humans, primates, and the great apes hug; the closest your dog hugs another is when the male clasps the female when mating or when a dog mounts another as a way to show their status.

Sense Games We often use the sense of touch, such as with a stroke on the head, as a way of reinforcing a good behaviour. However, if a dog is overly sensitive to touch, particularly around the head and neck area, where the collar and lead would be positioned, it is important that owners avoid distressing their dogs by handling them around this area.

Have Treats and Be Patient When teaching your dog new games and tricks, having great treats, using favourite toys, and being patient are the essentials to success.

Your dog does not know what you want him to do; you have to teach him. I have often heard many owners complain that their dog 'doesn't know how to fetch'. Most owners assume that because their dog is a particular breed such as a golden retriever, the dog should automatically know how to retrieve. Although some breeds do have a natural instinct to play 'fetch', it does not necessarily mean they will instinctively know what you want them to do!

There are lots of different treats you can use for game playing from kibble to carrots. I recommend you reserve your higher value foods such as cut-up sausage, liver cake, and so on for game playing or doing tricks in environments where there are more distractions like the park. This is because you are vying for your dog's attention from potential distractions such as other dogs, wildlife, joggers, cyclists, and the like. Your dog may become highly excitable when offered a piece of dried food in your front room, but when you step outside your front door, he may ignore the same food. Make sure your treats are healthy, so you are not compromising your pet's weight.

Play Time

Now you are fully prepared; let's look at some great game ideas for you and your dog. Most of these games can be played with dogs of all ages. However, some may involve a higher level of fitness or sharp movements which may not be suitable for an older or infirm dog, so I have categorised play ideas into sections—from pups, teenagers, adults to pensioners.

All the games test your dog's problem-solving ability, memory, language comprehension, observational skills, spatial awareness, fitness levels, and learning ability.

The Young Dog

Playing with your puppy will help to build his trust in humans, give him confidence, and help teach him what is and is not appropriate through play.

Which Pot Is It Under?

Wash out three large yogurt-type pots and have a handful of treats. Rub all three pots with the treat. (If you don't, your dog will simply follow his super-sensitive nose to the correct pot.) Sit opposite your dog and tell him to 'stay'. Show him the treat in your hand. Put it under one of the pots and repeat your 'stay' request. Mix the pots around as your dog watches. Stop moving the pots and say, 'Get it'. Your dog will topple all the pots, trying to find the magic one.

Chase Me

Your puppy is a natural predator, so incorporate hunting games into your play, such as 'chase me'. Call your dog by saying his name and 'Come!' in an excitable tone, use your body language to signal clearly to your dog what you want by clapping your hands, bending forward in a play bow, and turn your body sideways and start to move away. This action will lure your dog to race back to you. You can also throw your dog's favourite toy or treats behind you as you move away, as an extra sweetener to this chasing game. Practise this in an area where there are few distractions such as your garden and then increase the level of difficulty. This game reinforces recall and makes you more interesting than other distractions around you, such as other dogs and wildlife.

Let's Play Tug

Tugging games can be great fun for you and your dog and can act as a pain relief for a young, teething puppy. You can use rope toys or make your own by tying a knot in a damp tea towel. However, if your dog gets overly excited when playing tug, this may quickly turn from nice play to play gone wrong, which could lead to a bite. If your dog gets easily excited or shows any sign of aggressive behaviour during tugging games, it is best to avoid them.

Hunt the Treat

With a handful of treats, take your dog into a room. Have someone hold the dog while you hide treats around the rooms. Once you have finished, let him go and say, 'Go seek' or 'Find them'. If he needs help, lead him to the ones he has missed.

> **Paws for Thought** If your puppy starts to chew on your hands or clothing during play, transfer this chewing action onto something such as a rubberised toy and praise him when he chews on this instead. This teaches your puppy that hands and clothing are not toys.

For the Teenager

If your dog receives a treat for performing a task, it follows that he will repeat that task to ensure he is given another treat. However, sometimes, the exact task is not clear and you and your dog will have a different idea of what ensures a treat; for example, a dog that brings his toy to the owner may run away with it before the owner can reach for it. The owner may then move towards the dog in an attempt to get to the toy. The dog may find the owner's reaction much more enjoyable as he has successfully turned this into a game which he is dictating. Owners typically experience such behaviour when the dog reaches its teens. The games and tricks overleaf encourage specific skills.

eek

Put your dog into a 'sit-stay' or get someone to hold him in one room. Allow him to see you have treats with you. Hide from him in a closet, in a shower, behind a door, under the bed, in fact, anywhere! Once you are in your hiding place, call him. He will have to search throughout the house to find you. If he seems lost, call his name quietly from time to time. Once he finds you, show him you are happy, give him a treat, and praise. This game helps to test your dog's spatial awareness and language comprehension.

Dog Races

Take a small saucer and place it in a room or somewhere in the garden (the saucer makes the treat more visible). With your dog on the lead, take him to the plate and put a treat on it, but don't let him eat it. Lead the dog away from the treat. When you stop, ask him to 'sit'. The first few times you do this, keep your dog on the lead. In an excited way, say, 'Get the treat', and run with your dog to the treat. Make sure you win sometimes to keep the game challenging!

Retrieving

Catching and retrieving balls is a simple game, which many dogs enjoy. It tests your dog's reactions and obedience. Avoid throwing toys directly at your dog, as this can be dangerous as the ball could go down the dog's throat when caught. Instead, always throw the toy away from your dog.

Multiple Retrieving

If your dog really enjoys retrieving, then gather up several toys and place them in one area. Lead your dog away from the toy area and then give him your request, 'fetch'. He will race off to find one of his toys and bring it back to you. When he brings the toy back, take it, praise and reward, and then repeat the request, 'fetch'. If he is unsure what you want, lead him to the toy area and encourage him to pick up a toy and 'fetch' it back to you. With practice, your dog will learn to retrieve all the toys for you. Make sure you praise him each time!

Which Hand Is It In?

Have you ever seen a magician stuff a handkerchief into his fist and then ask the audience to guess which hand it is in, only to open up his hand and the hanky has disappeared? Well, this is the basic principle of this game. Make your hand into a fist and then place in it a strong, smelling, tasty treat. Let a little bit of the treat poke out of your hand and hold both fists in front of your dog's chest and ask him, 'Which hand?' If your dog sniffs at your hand holding the treat or paws at it, praise him and open your hand, so he gets the reward. If your dog gets it wrong, say, 'Uh-oh', and show him your hand to reveal that it is empty. Wait for a minute or two before repeating. Make sure you wash your hands before each go to reduce the smell of the treats on your hands which may confuse your dog. Vary the hand in which you have the treat. Once your dog is reliably choosing the correct hand, cover up the treat a little more until it is completely hidden.

Paws for Thought You should avoid teasing your dog deliberately or winding your dog up into a frenzy of excitement; this can be potentially dangerous and lead to a bite. Instead, you should wait for your dog to settle down and sit calmly waiting for, say his ball, before you start to play.

For the Adult

Now that your dog is fully grown, you can play more physical games that are more challenging!

Obstacle Race

Create your very own obstacle course race by setting up a few chairs in a large area such as your garden. Place a table or something you can both run under beyond the chairs and if you have a beanbag, or something you can climb over, include this in your course. Have a handful of treats and walk your dog through the course. Use this as an opportunity to reinforce heeling as you walk around, rewarding your dog with the food. After a few practices around the course, go a little faster and then keep increasing the speed day by day until you both are racing around. This is great exercise for you and your dog and in time, you will not even need to use your food reward.

Hula Hoop

To teach your dog this game, you need a circle-shaped object like a hula hoop, bicycle tyre, or alternatively, cut a piece of garden hose and tape it into a circle shape. Ensure you have some treats. With your dog in the sit position positioned to your left, pass his lead, so it is now in your right hand. Bend or kneel down, so your dog is close to your left hand side and pop a treat into your right hand and transfer the hoop to your left hand. Make sure the bottom of the hoop is just a couple of inches off the ground, so your dog is now facing the centre of the hoop. Lean forward and peer at the dog through the hoop and say, 'hoop', and use your treat to lure your dog through. He may be cautious at first, however, be patient. If your dog jumps or steps through the hoop, reward him with lots of praise and an edible reward.

Catch the Treat

Dogs have great vision when it comes to moving objects and a fantastic sense of smell; both of which will be needed in this game. Create a barrier between you and your dog; this can be approximately eight foot in length by two foot in width or you can mark out a line using tape on the ground. Your dog stays behind the barrier or line, while you stand a little way in front. Use a handful of treats to see how many he can catch in his mouth. Angle your hand so he has to run to the left and then to the right or the middle. Each time he catches a treat, praise him. To help your dog, look in the direction where you expect the treat to land, as he will be watching your hand position and eyes. If your dog has good observation skills, he will pick up on the cues from your eye movements.

Hurdles

Fetch a couple of buckets and a broom and balance the broom on the buckets at either end. Now you have created a make-shift hurdle. Start off with the jump at a low height and have some treats on you and a favourite toy or ball. Throw the toy over the hurdle and use your 'fetch' request. If your dog goes around the hurdle or under, simply call him back and start again. If your dog looks confused, you may want to show him what you want him to do by stepping over the hurdle and encouraging him to follow you. If your dog jumps over the hurdle, praise and reward him with your treats. Repeat this until your dog is reliably jumping over the hurdle. You can then start to raise the height of the jump. Make sure you take care to make it possible for your dog to jump. This is great exercise for your dog.

Play Frisbee

Catching a Frisbee and returning it is great fun for an active, healthy dog and enables him to use his chasing and pouncing instincts. Avoid throwing the Frisbee high in the air as this may encourage your dog to jump.

Jumping during catch games may damage your dog's joints, ligaments, and mouth, which is why this game is more suitable for the adult dog.

Pull Me

Some dogs have a higher desire to pull than others, such as the Siberian Husky, Alaskan Malamute, and Samoyed as these dogs were originally bred to pull sleds across long distances. You can exercise this using rollerblades, a sledge, or a little cart. When I was small, my brother and I would take it in turns to sit on a skateboard while the other ran in front of our family dog, holding a biscuit to encourage him. This was great fun; just make sure you do this in a safe and secure area and wear protective clothing and a cycling helmet in case you fall.

For the Pensioner

As our dogs grow older, they may be less capable of taking very rigorous exercise and play. However, games like 'what pot is it under?' are great for the elderly dog, as they exercise his brain and encourage the dog to use his scenting ability—the one sense that typically dogs never lose, while avoiding any physical stress to his joints and muscles.

Humans and dogs share a similar ageing process with arthritis, loss of hearing or sight, and organs becoming less efficient. Ageing can also affect them mentally as the structure of the nerve cells in the brain start to break down and connections from one cell to another may start to break, making the flow of information less efficient. It becomes hard for an old dog to learn new tricks. However, when a dog is provided with a healthy diet and a good balance of physical and mental activities, it is likely to have fewer or slow-progressing senile changes to the body and brain compared to an overweight, inactive dog.

As Smart as Rico

Test your dog's IQ with this memory game like Rico, the border collie. Make sure your dog knows the name of his favourite toy or buy a new toy and name it. Allow the dog to play with it using the toy's name, for example, 'Teddy'. Keep the toy in a particular area in the house or garden and when you give him the toy, say its name and give him a treat. After a few days of playing with the toy, leave the toy alone for a day. Then go to the area where the toy is usually left and ask your dog to 'fetch Teddy'. If he brings you the correct toy, praise and reward. If he gets it wrong, lead him back to the area and repeat. Use your eye movements and feet position to help direct him to the correct toy.

Smarter than Rico

Make this game more complex by naming several of your toys and allowing him to play with them each individually. After a few days, line all the toys up in a row. Ask your dog to 'fetch' one of his toys using that toy's name, as above. When your dog brings back the correct toy, repeat the request with a different toy's name until your dog has successfully retrieved all of the toys, picking out the correct ones by name.

The Betsy Challenge

Test your dog's skills like Betsy, another border collie, with a vocabulary of more than three hundred words and problem-solving ability. Place a new toy amongst your dog's group of named toys. Ask your dog to 'fetch' this new toy, giving it a name your dog has not heard before or doesn't recognise. See if your dog can use the process of elimination to pick out and bring you the correct new toy! If he looks confused, lead him back to the group of toys and repeat. If he brings you the correct toy immediately, your dog is a smart cookie so lavish him with praise and reward.

Uncover Me

While some dogs dig to bury toys or bones, others like to dig to create cool areas to lie in or may dig out of frustration. You can direct this in a positive way by providing your dog with a sandpit or specific flower bed in the garden. With your dog next to you, place his favourite toy or treat into the sandpit and dig at the area. Encourage your dog to copy your action by saying, 'dig' or 'where is it?' When your dog starts to dig and finds his toy or treat, then praise him.

How Do I Get It?

Test your dog's problem-solving ability by taking a piece of food reward or a favourite toy and place it under the sofa. Make sure it is far enough where he cannot reach it with his nose and tongue. See if your dog uses his paw to reach for it and he may bang his nose a few times before he works out to reach for it, using his paw. The quicker your dog works out how to retrieve it, the smarter he is.

Tricks for All Ages

Teaching your dog tricks is great fun for you and your dog and it helps him learn to listen to you. If your dog already knows the basics, such as 'sit', 'lie down', and 'stay', these are great building blocks for new tricks.

Paw

Pop your dog into a 'sit' and place a treat in your hand. Roll your hand into a ball and place it next to your dog's nose. Your dog will naturally sniff and want to get to the treat in your hand and when he raises his paw to get to your hand, praise him. Repeat this for five or six times and then introduce the word *paw* as he lifts his paw to your cupped hand. Repeat this for at least five more times and then begin to say,

'Paw', without the treat next to his nose. Praise and reward him when he gets it right.

High Five

Having mastered 'paw', now you can progress to 'high five'. Offer your hand as if to ask for paw, but when your dog lifts his paw, say, 'High five', and quickly turn your palm, so it is facing the dog, fingers pointing up; then praise and reward him. After several repetitions, as your dog starts to give you his paw, raise your hand slightly higher and higher and say, 'High five'. Keep raising your hand until your dog's paw is flat against yours and now you are 'high fiving'.

The Wave

To make things more challenging with the 'high five', why not teach your dog how to wave? Offer your hand out as if you are going to 'high five', as your dog goes to hit your palm with his paw, say, 'Wave'. Quickly withdraw your hand about three to six inches and wave hello/goodbye. Your dog should try to touch or swat your hand once or twice; when he does, praise and reward him.

Roll Over

Position your dog so he is lying down next to you and sit or kneel on the floor with a treat in your hand. Hold the treat close to your dog's nose then slowly move your hand so your dog turns his head to follow the treat. Give him the reward for watching the treat. Take another treat and move it further around, so that his head is now turning over his shoulder. Praise and reward him. Next move the treat right the way over your dog's shoulder, so he naturally falls to the side or rolls over as he attempts to follow the treat. When he rolls, say, 'Roll over' and then praise and reward him.

Sniff

This is an easy trick for your dog as he already knows how to do it. This trick is how to make your dog sniff on cue. Point at an object around the house and say, 'Sniff'. When your dog sniffs, praise and reward him. By repeating this exercise, your dog will be sniffing on cue and receiving huge enjoyment in investigating all the interesting aromas on household objects that he may never have been allowed to experience before.

Washing Day

Once your dog knows how to fetch, you can then have lots of fun with this trick. With your dog by your side, find a favourite soft toy or tea towel and throw this into the washing machine. If your dog sniffs at the machine, praise him and give him a treat. If he looks at you confused, encourage him to look for the chosen item by tossing in a treat. If he pops his head into the machine without having retrieved anything, throw in some treats to encourage him to fetch the item. If he picks up the item, wait until his head is out of the machine and then give him lots of praise and several treats. When you reach the point where your dog is retrieving the item reliably, you can add a word to help him connect with this action. I suggest you use the same one you use for any retrieving such as 'fetch'.

How Embarrassing!

You will need a cushion, a folded towel, or something that your dog can push his nose under. Show your dog a treat. Put your hand holding the treat under the cushion and make sure the cushion is near his nose, so he can smell the treat. As your dog finds it, praise him and let him eat it. After a few repetitions, your dog should start to become more enthusiastic as he stuffs his nose under the cushion to get to the treat. As he starts doing this, say, 'How embarrassing!' After more repetitions, begin to move the treat back further towards the rear of the cushion, so you are encouraging your dog to put his entire head under it. With practice and patience, all you will need to say is, 'How embarrassing!' and your dog will automatically pop his head under a pillow or cushion.

Shut That Drawer!

Open a drawer slightly and call your dog to come to you. Have treats ready and attract your dog's attention by placing the food reward onto the front section of the open drawer. If your dog nudges at the food to reach it, praise and reward him. Repeat this again and if he manages to move the drawer shut, give your dog lots of praise and his treats. If your dog looks confused, you can help him out by wiping something tasty onto the drawer to encourage him to touch it. Once your dog gets the hang of what you want, then start to introduce a cue such as 'Close it' as the dog touches the drawer.

Shut the Door

Make sure you have a door that swings easily on its hinges and have a handful of treats. Open the door a few inches and then balance a treat on the door handle, making sure your dog is in a 'sit/stay' position watching you. Attract your dog's attention to the treat and say, 'Shut the door'. Encourage him to reach for the treat using his front paw on the door; this should close it. The treat will fall off the handle as the door shuts, enabling your dog to eat it, and then praise him. Practise this at least five or six times then you can make it harder by popping the treat on the door handle while he is in another room. Call your dog and say, 'Shut the door', and use your eye movements and the position of your feet to direct him towards the door. If he looks confused, lead him to the door and show him the treat, encouraging him to retrieve it. Once your dog has successfully mastered this, teach your dog to shut the door without having a treat visible. As soon as he does shut the door on request, give your dog the treat and lots of praise.

Drop on Cue

If your dog knows how to lie down, you can advance to teaching him this trick. Call your dog to your side with treats in your hand. Walk forward a few paces at a slow pace then show him your signal for lying down and at the same time, say, 'Down'.

Back Up

Call your dog to you, so you are standing in front of him. Slowly walk towards him, encouraging him to step backwards. As he starts to go back, say, 'Back up' and praise and reward him when he gets it right. If your dog backs up sideways, start again. Some dogs find it easier to learn this trick when you stand next to them. So, stand just a little ahead of your dog, with him at the side of you. As you move backwards, move your arm backwards towards your dog, so your hand is fairly close to his face. This will help to direct him backwards. Praise and reward him when he gets it right.

Through the Legs

Pop your dog into a 'sit' position then stand in front of him and stretch your legs apart, so he can fit through the gap. Have some treats in your hand, show your dog the treat, bend forward, and then throw the treat backwards, so it falls through your legs and a little way beyond. As your dog runs through your legs say, 'Through'. Give him lots of praise and another treat.

Weaving

Like 'through the legs', this trick is great to use as part of a dog dance routine! Have your dog on his lead then step forward. Slowly pass the lead between your legs, have a treat in your other hand, and show this to your dog. Using the treat as an incentive, encourage your dog to follow the treat, so he walks through the gap. Step forward again, this time on your other leg, and repeat. In time, you can stop using the lead and build up the pace of your movements so your dog is smoothly weaving through your legs with each step forward.

Spin and Twist

Have a treat in your hand and show it to your dog. Move the hand holding the treat in a wide circle motion to the left and say, 'Spin', to encourage your dog to move around. Reward him and give him lots of praise. To teach the 'twist' simply, change the direction of your hand, so it is circling to the right. By repeating and practising this, you will not have to use the treat as an incentive.

Away

You will need to use a towel or blanket. Lay the towel on the floor, a good distance away from you. Pop your dog on his lead and say, 'Away', as you run to the towel. When you reach the towel, touch it and say, 'Down'. The towel acts as a marker for where you want him to be. After a few repetitions, see if your dog can go to the towel by himself on your cue. Once your dog gets the idea of 'away', begin to make the towel smaller by folding it up until you no longer need it.

Bobbing for Balls

If you have ever played the apple-bobbing game at Halloween, you will understand the principle of this trick. Drop several toys or balls into a bucket. Let your dog stick his nose into the bucket to have a sniff or a look. When he does this, encourage him to take one of the balls or toys by saying, 'Take it'. You may at first have to give him the ball to help him understand what you want him to do. Once your dog has the general idea, add some water to make this more challenging; this is great for problem solving.

Let's Tidy Up

If you use a container to keep your dog's toys in, you will need it for this trick. Place the toy basket in the middle of a room and kneel down beside it. Place the toys around the basket and ask your dog to 'fetch' one of the toys. When he picks up the toy, hold the basket underneath his jaw and say, 'Tidy up'. If he drops it into the basket, praise and reward him. If your dog looks confused, ask him to 'drop' and praise him when he drops it into the basket. Practise this five or six times and change your cue word to 'tidy up'.

Watch Me

This is a useful request to teach your dog, especially, if he is easily distracted by the sight of another dog or wildlife when out on a walk. Call your dog to you and pop him into a 'sit' in front of you. Hold a treat and show it to him in your hand and then bring it close to your face and say, 'Watch me'. Look directly at the dog and as soon as he makes eye contact, reward and praise him. With lots of practice and by slowly introducing distractions, you will be able to make your dog look at you automatically without asking for the 'watch me' rather than looking at the interesting squirrel racing across the park.

Take a Bow

With your dog sitting next to you, offer him a treat, so his head dips down to take it. As he does this, praise and reward him. If he goes to lie down as he takes the treat or thinks you are asking for a 'lie down', say, 'Uh-oh', and try again. Once your dog has the idea and is dipping his head down then ask him to give you his paw. However, pop your hand on the ground so he has to stretch forward to touch it. When he touches your hand, give your dog praise and reward him. Having mastered this stage, you can now move onto combining the two movements. Hold the treat low to the ground and just out of reach so your dog dips his head down and moves his leg towards your hand. As he does this say, 'Bow', and give him lots of praise and reward when he gets it right.

Group Activities—Play Mates

There has been a growing trend for group classes based on activities such as agility, fly ball, obedience, and dog dancing. These activities can be great fun and a good way for you and your dog to stay fit and learn to work as a team. Not all dogs enjoy group classes, as some dogs may be less confident with lots of noise or when amongst strangers or groups of dogs. Take your dog's temperament as well as his age, level of health, and fitness into account because what you think might be fun and enjoyable may not be for your dog.

Agility Classes

The course, usually outside, presents the dog with a number of different obstacles to negotiate around, under, through, and over. These may include planks, hoops, and tunnels. This can be a great workout and provides good mental stimulation.

Fly Ball

This involves the dog making a number of jumps before he reaches a platform, where he is trained to press a pedal to release a ball and then race back to the owner with the ball.

Obedience Classes

Look for classes in your local area that focus on positive reinforcement and are fun. Avoid old-fashioned trainers who use punishment and force as a means of control. Most trainers will welcome anyone interested in joining their classes to come along and watch. This will give you a feel for whether it is the right class for you and your dog.

Dog Dancing

This is the ultimate activity for teamwork as you learn to dance in a choreographed routine with your dog, which is set to music. Owners can heel to music or dance freestyle. One of the best known trainers for her fantastic dog-dancing routines is Mary Ray, who is a regular at Crufts. More dog dancing classes have been established, but if you cannot find one in your local area, why not start your own dog dance troupe?

Sledding

Dog sledding or 'mushing' is when a team of dogs is harnessed up and attached to a wheeled rig or sled, which they then have to pull. Dog sledding has become a popular winter recreation and sport across North America and Europe in recent years, where teams race against one another. Check the Internet for more specific information about sled dog racing and the equipment used, both recreational and competitive, such as www.sleddogcentral.com or the International Sled Dog Racing Association.

Toys

Shop-Bought

There are hundreds of toys available to buy for your dog—a wide range
of toys of different shapes, sizes, and textures is far more stimulating
to him than having several balls. Buying new toys or even rotating your

dog's toys as well as varying the types of games played will help to enrich his life. Kongs and Buster Cubes with treats placed inside the hollow centre are a great way to keep a dog busy if he is left on his own, as he has to problem solve, helping to relieve stress and boredom. There are also a number of wooden, puzzle toys available, where treats can be hidden, and the dog has to work out how to dispense the treat using his paw and nose to move the toy around or pull the lever.

Rope toys are great for playing tug, and like rubberised toys, they can help ease discomfort for a teething, young dog when chewing on them. Make sure you buy the right size for your dog as a larger breed will need a larger rope toy.

Playing Frisbee is a great way to keep your dog fit and put his hunting instinct to good use. Avoid hard plastic Frisbees as these could break off or splinter if your dog chews or bites down hard on them. Instead, choose Frisbees specifically marketed at dogs, such as the Kong Frisbee made out of rubber.

Nearly all dogs like a toy that squeaks and seem to get even more enjoyment out of 'killing' the squeak, so do make sure you have a few toys in your dog's collection that he can throw around, shake, and pierce through the squeak as he acts out his natural predatory behaviour.

Making Your Own

It can be fun and cost-effective to make your own toys for your dog. For example, plastic drinks bottles make great alternatives to Buster Cubes and Kongs, by washing out a bottle and perforating it with holes the size of your dog's dried food or treats. Place some treats or your dog's kibble into the bottle and watch your dog work out how to roll the bottle to make the food come out. You can also use items like old socks knotted together (make sure they are large enough so your dog cannot swallow them) or an old tea towel, dampened and knotted in the middle to make a great alternative to the rope toy. Dogs love investigating new items of differing shapes and textures, so wash plastic milk jugs or containers and let him play around with these. Cardboard boxes are a cheap way to entertain your dog. Stuff a box with old rags and place it on its side and then place a treat or favourite toy towards the back of the box. Watch your dog enjoy digging and scenting his way through to get to that all important reward. You can also use garden objects like bamboo canes to create your own agility course, where your dog has to weave around the canes, and an old rubber dustbin with the bottom cut out makes a great tunnel.

> **Paws for Thought** Choose toys that are safe, ideally a little too large for the puppy to swallow them, and if they are soft toys, ensure eyes/tails/ears or any other attachable sections are firmly fixed. Avoid giving your dog children's soft toys, as the stuffing is likely to be covered in a flame-resistant coating, which, if consumed by your dog, could be highly toxic.

It's Not All Fun and Games

Tips to Remember

Keep it short. You do not have to play for hours with your dog to make him a happy hound. Play or do your tricks in short bursts; that way, it stays fun for you both.

Play biting. Dogs, especially puppies, learn vital information about what they can and cannot get away with through play. Young dogs tend to bite during play as they are still learning about bite control. If your puppy bites you by accident during a game, let out a loud and high-pitched 'yelp' and then move away from the puppy. This shows your dog the bite was painful and the game has ceased as a result. Be patient and consistent with this; in time, your puppy will learn to inhibit his bite.

Don't tease. Avoid deliberately teasing or winding your dog up into a frenzy of excitement as this can easily turn from nice play to play gone wrong where the dog's frustration leads to aggressive behaviour and a bite. Instead, wait for your dog to settle down and sit calmly before you throw his ball.

Avoid rough and tumble. Some dog owners enjoy playing roughly with their dogs or wrestling around with them. However, it is best to avoid these games altogether as your dog will not understand the difference in playing roughly with an adult to a child and this could lead to your dog becoming overzealous and thinking it is acceptable to jump on you or mouth you.

If you have children, teach them what is and what is not appropriate play.

Play Time Is Over

While it can be endearing to watch your dog play enthusiastically with children, it is important to recognise the difference between 'enthusiastic play' and potentially threatening or dangerous behaviour. Some dogs, especially teenagers, can become easily excited or aroused during play as they find it more challenging to regulate their emotions. Knowing the signs to look out for is important to avoid a potentially dangerous situation—prevention is better than cure. The best way to understand what to look out for is by watching your dog and learning his typical body postures, facial expressions and vocalisations during play. Many dogs, like mine, will bark during a game of 'fetch' as if to say, 'This is so much fun!' while other dogs may play-growl. Once you are familiar with your dog's movements, expressions, and vocalisations, you will be more aware of when he is becoming overly excited.

Signs to Look out For

- Movements become faster and less coordinated; for example, leaping is higher or he is racing around and getting himself into a spin
- Barking becomes louder, higher pitched, and in quick succession
- If your dog play-growls, the growling may change to a lower pitch and will sound more menacing
- Jumping or leaping up at you
- Nipping at your clothes or arm
- He uses his head or body to punch into you
- Mouth becomes retracted so you can see some teeth—this looks similar to a pant
- Eyes become fixed/rounded, almost as if he is staring
- Dog stops playing and his body stiffens. This can be a warning that a bite could be imminent.

If you notice any of these, you should stop playing and break the state through distraction either by asking your dog to 'sit' or 'lie down' or ask for a 'paw', as this encourages him into a cognitive state and calms him down. Alternatively, say something like 'Dinner time' or 'Let's go for a walk' and calmly walk away.

If you teach your dog when 'enough is enough', you can help to avoid any risks. To teach your dog this, you need to give him a signal which means that play time has ended. Start by engaging your dog in a game and throw his favourite toy or play 'tug'. Once he is enjoying the game, say, 'All done' or 'Enough now'. Make sure you use a calm, low, and quiet voice and change your body posture, so you are standing upright, turn slightly, and look away from your dog. Stay calm, still, and quiet for a moment. This clear visual and verbal signal shows your dog something has changed in this situation. Your dog may also stop playing and stand still, wondering what is about to happen next. If he does this, immediately praise and reward him in a calming manner, so you do not excite your dog and then start the game all over again. If your dog is confused when you stop playing and does not react to your change of behaviour, turn and walk away slowly. This makes it clear that the game is over. Some dogs will pause as you do this, so now you can praise him for his calm and quiet behaviour and become used to ending all your game or trick sessions with the words *'all done'* or *'enough now.'*

Now, go and have some fun with your dog!

References

Abrantes, R. 2005. *The Evolution of Canine Social Behaviour*. Washington: Wakan Tanka Publishers.

Beaver, B. 2009. *Canine Behaviour Insights and Answers*. St Louis: Saunders Elsevier.

Coren, S. 2005. *How Dogs Think*. London: Pocket Books.Coren, S. 2007. *Why Does My Dog Act That Way?* London: Pocket Books.

Fisher, John. 2005. *Think Dog! An Owner's Guide to Canine Psychology*. London: Octopus Publishing Group Ltd.

Fogle, B. 1990. *The Dog's Mind*. London: Pelham Books.

Lindsay, S. 2000. *Handbook of Applied Dog Behavior and Training*. Ames: Blackwell Publishing.

McConnell, P. 2002. *The Other End of the Leash*. New York: Ballantine Books, The Random House Publishing Group.

McConnell, P. 2008. *Play Together, Stay Together*. Black Earth: McConnell Publishing Limited.

McMillan, F. 2005. *Mental Health and Well-Being in Animals*. New Jersey: Wiley-Blackwell.

Morell, V. 2008. *Minds of Their Own*, Tampa: National Geographic.

Turner, T. 2006. *Veterinary Notes for Dog Owners.* London: Popular Dogs Publishing.

Woodcock, D. 2002. *Preventing Puppy Problems; Live in Peace with Your Puppy*. Reading: Dogsense Publications.

Wynne, C. 2004. *Does Your Dog Understand You?* www.the-scientist.com/article/display/15156/ (Last accessed: June 11, 2010).

Lightning Source UK Ltd.
Milton Keynes UK
UKHW010638230421
382498UK00001B/74